RUGBY
TO
STAFFORD

Vic Mitchell and Keith Smith

MP Middleton Press

Front cover: Arriving at Polesworth on 4th June 1963 is 4-6-0 no. 75016 with the 5.28pm Coventry to Tamworth service. The electrification work had started recently. (H.Ballantyne)

Back cover upper: No. 304028 is working an up local service on 17th May 1980 and is seen from Polesworth signal box. This is featured on the front cover. (A.C.Hartless)

Back cover lower: Emerging from Shugborough Tunnel on 23rd June 1988 is no. 86245 Dudley Castle *with the 16.20 Euston to Liverpool "Merseyside Pullman". (H.Ballantyne)*

Published November 2011

ISBN 978 1 908174 07 9

© Middleton Press, 2011

Design Deborah Esher

Published by
    Middleton Press
    Easebourne Lane
    Midhurst
    West Sussex
    GU29 9AZ
Tel: 01730 813169
Fax: 01730 812601
Email: info@middletonpress.co.uk
www.middletonpress.co.uk

Printed in the United Kingdom by Henry Ling Limited, at the Dorset Press, Dorchester, DT1 1HD

INDEX

ACKNOWLEDGEMENTS

We are very grateful for the assistance received from many of those mentioned in the credits also to B. Bennett, A.R.Carder, G.Croughton, J.B.Horne, S.C.Jenkins, J.P.McCrickard, B.Lewis, B.I.Nathan, Mr D. and Dr S.Salter, M.Turvey, T.Walsh and especially our ever supportive wives, Barbara Mitchell and Janet Smith.

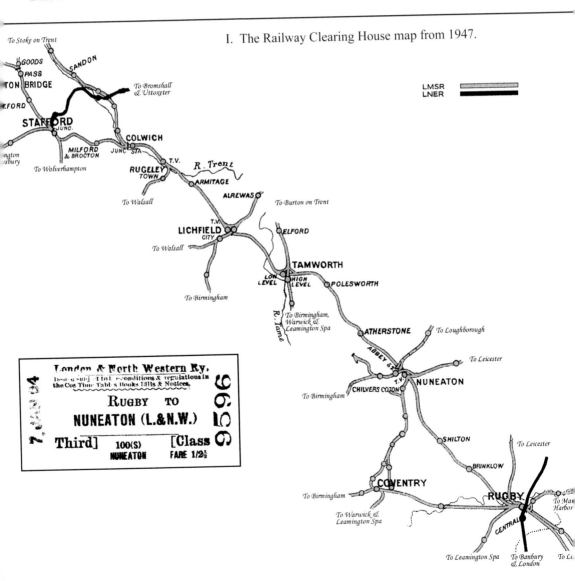

I. The Railway Clearing House map from 1947.

GEOGRAPHICAL SETTING

The ancient trading and educational centre of Rugby is at the confluence of the west flowing River Avon and the south flowing River Swift. The former gains fame at Stratford and passes under our route about one mile west of the station. The route runs close to the Oxford Canal for about six miles, the waterway linking Oxford with Coventry.

Rugby is on the northern extension of the Cotswold Hills and their limestone underlies railways in this area. Further north, our route runs close to the northern border of the coalfield which runs north from Coventry. It extends from Nuneaton to Tamworth, but has not been productive in recent years. Between these places, the route is close to the River Anker, which flows northwest.

At Tamworth, the line enters the valley of the River Tame and passes over it before following the sinuous course of the Birmingham & Fazeley Canal for a short distance towards Lichfield. The Trent Valley is reached at Armitage, along with the Trent & Mersey Canal. Both are followed through Rugeley to Colwich.

Shugborough Tunnel takes the line through a small ridge of sandstone and it then enters the valley of the River Sow to reach Stafford, passing over the River Penk in the process. This historic market town is an important commercial and manufacturing centre.

The first section of the route is in the northern part of Warwickshire. The line passes into Staffordshire near the northern border of Tamworth.

The maps are to the scale of 25ins to 1 mile, with north at the top, unless otherwise indicated.

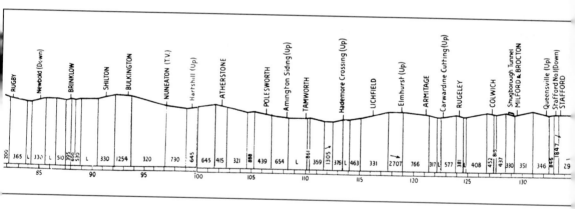

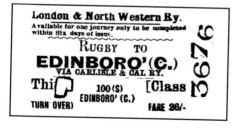

HISTORICAL BACKGROUND

The London & Birmingham Railway was opened between Euston and Birmingham in 1838 and it became the first part of the London & North Western Railway in 1846. The line was extended to Stafford on 15th September 1847, where it met the Grand Junction Railway, which had opened from Liverpool in 1837. It formed the northern part of the LNWR in 1846.

From Rugby trains ran to Birmingham from 1838, to Leicester from 1840 (to 1962), to Market Harborough from 1850 (to 1966), to Leamington from 1851 (to 1959) and to Northampton from 1881.

From Nuneaton there were services to Coventry from 1850, to Hinckley from 1862, to Whitacre from 1864 (to 1968) and to Ashby from 1873 (to 1931).

From Tamworth one could travel south towards Birmingham from 1839 and north to Derby from the same year.

From Lichfield trains operated to Walsall and also to Derby from 1849, but the latter ended in 1965.

One could travel south from Rugeley Trent Valley from 1859 (to 1965) to reach Walsall and again from 1998.

The route from Colwich to Stone opened in 1849.

Stafford had links west to Wellington from 1849 (to 1964) and east to Uttoxeter from 1867 (to 1939). The figures in brackets refer mainly to local passenger services. The GJR route south to Birmingham via Wolverhampton opened in 1837.

The LNWR became a constituent of the London Midland & Scottish Railway in 1923. Its area formed the London Midland Region of British Railways upon nationalisation in 1948. In 1986, most main line traffic went into the InterCity sector.

The name "North London Railways" was applied from 31st March 1994 to the services to Birmingham via Northampton. These were named Silverlink Trains after privatisation on 2nd March 1997, when a 7½ year franchise was taken by the National Express Group. A week later, Virgin West Coast Trains took over main line operations, with the exception of ScotRail sleeper services, on a 15 year franchise.

Central Trains operated local trains on the route from 2nd March 1997, London Midland taking over on 11th November 2007.

ELECTRIFICATION

25,000 volt AC electrification extended in stages south from Stafford.

Lichfield - Stafford	22 October 1963
Nuneaton - Lichfield	2 March 1964
Rugby - Nuneaton	16 November 1964
London Euston - Manchester/Liverpool	18 April 1966
full accelerated electric services.	

WIDENING

Rugby - Trent Valley Junction	1885
Trent Valley Junction - Nuneaton Up line	1871/3
Trent Valley Junction - Brinklow Down line	1906
Attleborough - Nuneaton Down line	1910
Nuneaton - Atherstone	1909/10
Atherstone - Tamworth	1901/3
Tamworth - Armitage	2008
Armitage - Rugeley	1913
Rugeley - Colwich	1902/3
Milford & Brocton - Stafford	1898

Brinklow - Attleborough (Nuneaton) only ever had three lines; no Down Slow due to the proximity of the Oxford Canal. Similarly, Colwich - Milford & Brocton remained two track because of the expense of providing a second tunnel at Shugborough.

PASSENGER SERVICES

The table below gives an indication of the frequency of services. **Fast** refers to trains running non-stop between Rugby and Stafford: **Semi-fast** are those calling at the main intermediate stations, while **Stopping** means most stations. Short workings are not included.

	Fast		Semi-fast		Stopping	
	Weekdays	Sundays	Weekdays	Sundays	Weekdays	Sundays
1850	0	0	3	2	3	1
1876	0	0	9	4	5	0
1901	1	1	7	4	2	0
1925	5	3	3	3	5	0
1950	6	4	4	2	3	1
1975	7	3	1	2	6*	0
2000	0	0	16	8	4*	0

* By this time most local trains ran from Coventry and joined the route at Nuneaton.

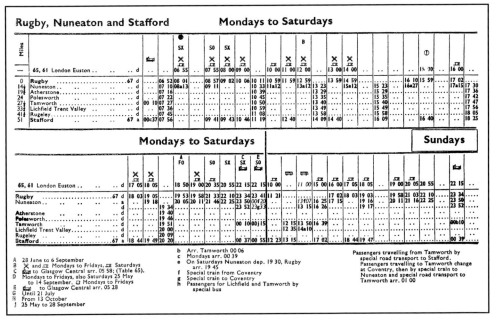

May 1974

Rugby and Coventry → Nuneaton and Stafford

Mondays to Fridays

Miles																								
		VT	VT	CT		VT	VT	VT		VT	CT	VT		VT	VT	CT		VT	VT	VT		VT	CT	VT
		MO	MO																					
		■1 ◇	■1 ◇			■1 ◇	■1 ◇	■1 ◇		■1 ◇		■1 ◇		■1 ◇	■1 ◇			■1 ◇	■1 ◇	■1 ◇		■1 ◇		■1 ◇
		A	A																					
		🛒	🛒			⊠	⊠	⊠		⊠		⊠		⊠	⊠			🛒	✕	🛒		🛒		⊠
0	London Euston [15] ⊖ 65, 66 d	22p43	23p43			06 05	06 28	07 28		07 58		08 58		09 23	09 33	08b43		09 58	10 23	11 33		11 58		12 58
82½	**Rugby** 65 d	00 09	01 09			07 12	07 33	08 41						10 24	10 38				11 31	12 35				
94	**Coventry** 58 d			05 33		05 33				08c23						10 30						12 30		13 30
100½	Bedworth 58 d			05 44																				
104	**Nuneaton** 58, 65 d	00s21	01s21	05 52		07 27	07 47			09 14	09 49			10a36		11 12		11 18	11a43			13 12	13 25	14 12
109	Atherstone d			05 58							09 55					11 18							13 31	
113	Polesworth d			06 04							10 01					11 24							13 37	
116½	Tamworth Low Level d			06 09		07a39	08 00				10 07				11a00	11 30				12a57			13 43	
122¾	Lichfield Trent Valley d			06 17				09a06			10a14	10 25				11 38							13 55	
130¾	Rugeley Trent Valley 70 d			06 28												11 56							14 06	
140	**Stafford** 70 a			06 40			08 21			09 43		10 41				12 10		11 45				13 41	14 21	14 41

	VT	VT		VT	VT	VT		CT	VT	VT		VT	VT	VT		VT	VT	VT	VT	VT	VT	VT		
																					FO			
	■1 ◇	■1 ◇		■1 ◇	■1 ◇	■1 ◇			■1 ◇	■1 ◇		■1 ◇	■1 ◇	■1 ◇		■1 ◇	■1 ◇	■1 ◇	■1 ◇	■1 ◇	■1 ◇	■1 ◇		
								B		C						D					D			
	🛒	🛒		🛒	🛒	🛒			⊠	🛒		⊠	🛒	🛒		🛒	🛒	⊠	🛒	🛒	🛒	🛒		
London Euston [15] ⊖ 65, 66 d	13 33	13 58		14 58	15 33	16 03		15 38	16 53	17 23		17 53	18 38	18 58		19 18	19 33	19 58	20 33	21 03	21 08	22 05		
Rugby 65 d	14 35	15 01			16 41					18 33			19 45				20 38		21 41		22 17	23 29		
Coventry 58 d		14 30		15 30		16 30		17 15						19 30								22 10		
Bedworth 58 d								17 26																
Nuneaton 58, 65 d		15 17		16 13		17 12		17 38	18a07			19a07		20 15		20 33		21 17		22 14	22 31	23 43		
Atherstone d								17 45																
Polesworth d								17 51																
Tamworth Low Level d	14 58				17a04			18 01		18 55			20 07				20a59		22 03					
Lichfield Trent Valley d	15a05							18 09		19a02			20 16						22a10					
Rugeley Trent Valley 70 d								18 20																
Stafford 70 a		15 46		16 41		17 42		18 40					20 32	20 43		21 00		21 45		22 41	22 58	00 12		

Saturdays

	CT	VT		VT	VT		VT	CT		VT	VT		CT	VT		VT	VT		VT	VT		CT	VT	VT
		■1 ◇		■1 ◇	■1 ◇		■1 ◇			■1 ◇	■1 ◇			■1 ◇		■1 ◇	■1 ◇		■1 ◇	■1 ◇			■1 ◇	■1 ◇
		🛒		🛒	🛒		🛒			🛒	🛒			🛒		🛒	🛒		🛒	🛒			🛒	🛒
London Euston [15] ⊖ 65, 66 d		06 16		07 18	07 43		07 53			08 53	09 18		08b28	09 53		09 58	10 53		11 13	11 53			12 53	13 18
Rugby 65 d		07 32		08 43			09 16				10 35			11 05		11 20			12 27					14 35
Coventry 58 d					08 24					09 30			10 30				11 30			12 30			13 30	
Bedworth 58 d																								
Nuneaton 58, 65 d	05 52	07 46			09 15		09 30	09 40		10 15			11 15	11 19		11 34	12 18			13 15		13 32	14 18	
Atherstone d	05 58							09 46					11 21									13 39		
Polesworth d	06 04							09 52					11 27									13 44		
Tamworth Low Level d	06 09	07 58						09 58			10a57		11 34						12a49			13 53		14 57
Lichfield Trent Valley d	06 17			09a07				10a05					11 42			11a48						14 01		15a05
Rugeley Trent Valley 70 d	06 28												11 59									14 19		
Stafford 70 a	06 39	08 18			09 44		09 58			10 42			12 11	11 45			12 46			13 42		14 37	14 44	

	VT		VT	VT		VT	VT		CT	VT		VT	VT		VT	VT		VT	VT		VT			
	■1 ◇		■1 ◇	■1 ◇		■1 ◇	■1 ◇			■1 ◇		■1 ◇	■1 ◇		■1 ◇	■1 ◇		■1 ◇	■1 ◇		■1 ◇			
									B				D								E			
	🛒		🛒	🛒		🛒	🛒			🛒		🛒	🛒		🛒	🛒		🛒	🛒		🛒			
London Euston [15] ⊖ 65, 66 d	13 53		14 53	15 18		15 38	15 53		15 28	16 53		17 53	17 58		18 38	18 48		19 18	19 43		21 53			
Rugby 65 d	15 06			16 41														20 46			23 23			
Coventry 58 d	14 30		15 30				16 32		17 15			18 30				19 30					22 02			
Bedworth 58 d									17 26															
Nuneaton 58, 65 d	15 20		16 18				17 14		17 38	18 17		19 14				20 18					23 37			
Atherstone d									17 44															
Polesworth d									17 50															
Tamworth Low Level d				17a03					17 59				19 36						21 45					
Lichfield Trent Valley d						17 13			18 07						20 14			21a11						
Rugeley Trent Valley 70 d									18 18															
Stafford 70 a	15 45		16 44			17 29	17 41		18 34	18 45		19 41	19 56		20 30	20 44			22 06		00 06			

Sundays

	VT	VT	VT	VT	VT	VT		VT	VT	VT	VT	VT	VT		VT	VT	VT	VT	VT	VT		VT	VT	VT
	■1 ◇	■1 ◇	■1 ◇	■1 ◇	■1 ◇	■1 ◇		■1 ◇	■1 ◇	■1 ◇	■1 ◇	■1 ◇	■1 ◇		■1 ◇	■1 ◇	■1 ◇	■1 ◇	■1 ◇	■1 ◇		■1 ◇	■1 ◇	■1 ◇
	G	G	G	G	G	G		G	G	G	H	G	G			G			G			G		G
	🛒	🛒	🛒	🛒	🛒	🛒		🛒	🛒	🛒	🛒	🛒	🛒		🛒	🛒	🛒	🛒	🛒	🛒		🛒	🛒	🛒
London Euston [15] ⊖ 65, 66 d	07 33	07 58	08 33	09 33	10 03	10 33		11 33	12 03	12 33	13 03	13 03	13 33		14 03	14 43	15 03	15 33	15 43	16 03		16 43	17 03	17 13
Rugby 65 d	09 05	09 35	10 05	11 05	11 36	12 05		13 05	13 34	14 05	14 22	14 28			15 17	16 00		16 43				17 56		
Coventry 58 d		08e30			11 23				13 00						13 56		15 14			16 12			17 15	
Bedworth 58 d																								
Nuneaton 58, 65 d	09a17	09 49	10a17	11a17	11 50	12a17		13a17	13 48	14a17			15a04		15 31	16a12	16 22		17a07	17 22		18a08	18 22	18a33
Atherstone d																								
Polesworth d																								
Tamworth Low Level d											14 45	14 50						17a04						
Lichfield Trent Valley d															15 46									
Rugeley Trent Valley 70 d																								
Stafford 70 a		10 16			12 17				14 15		15 10	15 12			16 07		16 54			17 54			18 54	

For general notes see front of timetable

- **A** Until 17 July
- **B** To Stoke-on-Trent (Table 68)
- **C** **Y Ddraig Gymreig/The Welsh Dragon**
- **D** **The Irish Mail**
- **E** Until 15 July and 23 September
- **G** Until 16 July
- **H** From 23 July
- **b** Change at Coventry and Nuneaton
- **c** Thursday 10 August to Monday 28 August dep. 0820
- **e** By bus

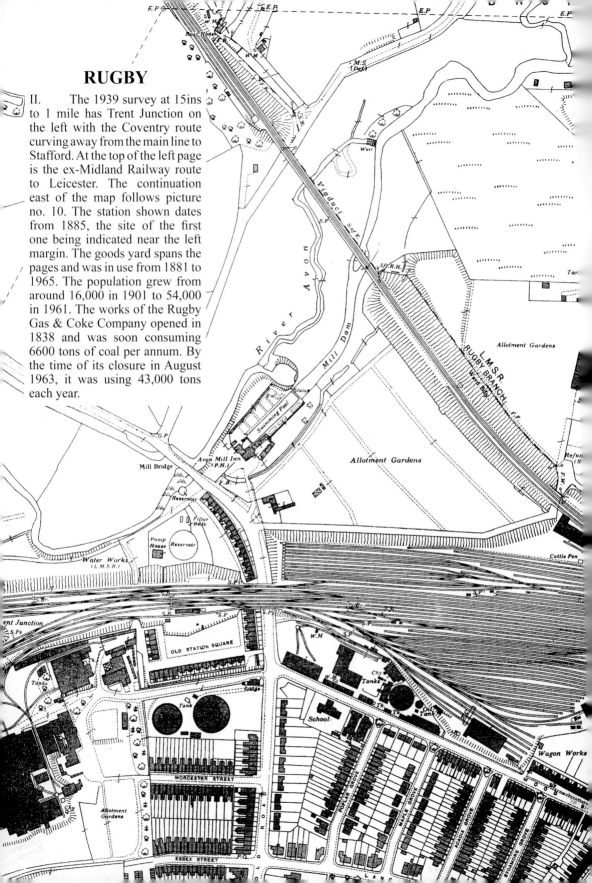

RUGBY

II.   The 1939 survey at 15ins to 1 mile has Trent Junction on the left with the Coventry route curving away from the main line to Stafford. At the top of the left page is the ex-Midland Railway route to Leicester. The continuation east of the map follows picture no. 10. The station shown dates from 1885, the site of the first one being indicated near the left margin. The goods yard spans the pages and was in use from 1881 to 1965. The population grew from around 16,000 in 1901 to 54,000 in 1961. The works of the Rugby Gas & Coke Company opened in 1838 and was soon consuming 6600 tons of coal per annum. By the time of its closure in August 1963, it was using 43,000 tons each year.

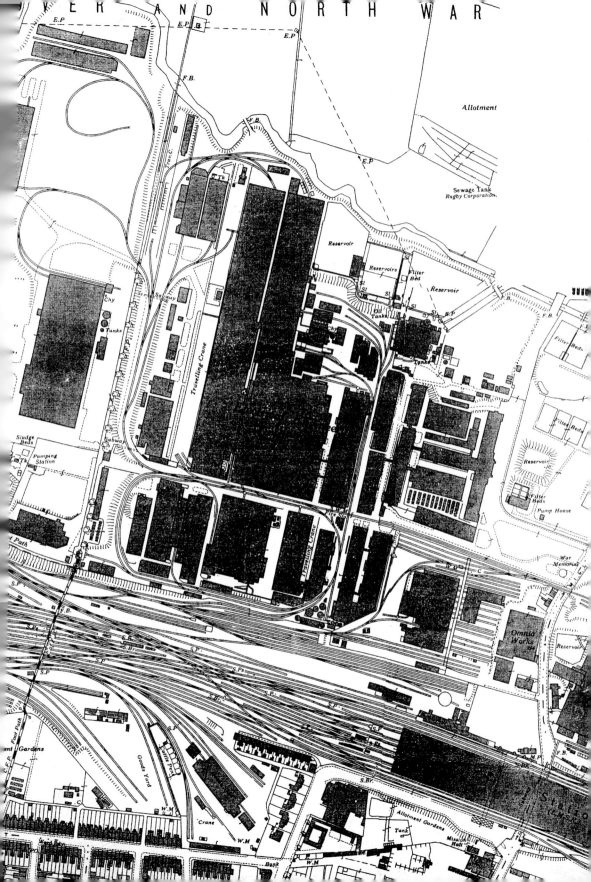

1.   Our earliest view is of an up train in 1904, headed by 4-4-0 no. 510 *Albatross*, soon after it was built at Crewe. A smoke deflector can be seen under the 1885 roof. Most engines of expresses were changed here until about 1880. (R.S.Carpenter coll.)

2.   An eastward panorama from the footbridge in about 1952 has the goods yard on the right and 4-6-2 no. 46243 *City of Lancaster* with an express for the North. On the left is the ex-MR engine shed and No. 5 Box. (Milepost 92½)

3.   Seen at the same time is an elliptical roof slip coach and No. 2 Box (32 levers), which was at the east end of the station on the down side. It closed along with the other remaining mechanical boxes in the station area (Nos 1,2,3,4,5 and 7) on 13th September 1964, the new power box taking over control the following day. No. 6 box had closed in 1939. (Milepost 92½)

D1.   Diagram to show the arrangement of routes around 1960. The water troughs would soon disappear and the nearby flyover for trains from Birmingham was new. (N.Langridge)

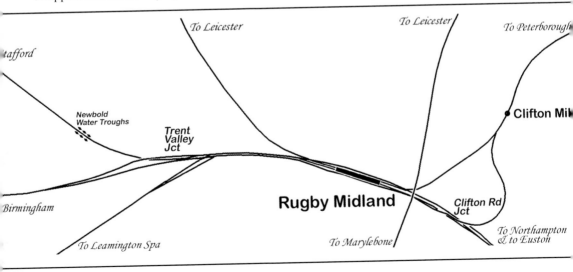

4.   We look west from the footbridge (near the join of the pages of map II) in around 1958, as a "Jubilee" class is approaching with an express bound for Euston. The up line from Coventry was provided with a flyover across the Trent Valley route from 17th September 1962. (Milepost 92½)

5.   Class 40 no. D233 is passing through with the up "Royal Scot" on 15th August 1962. The sign AEI indicates Associated Electrical Industries, the size of their premises being shown on the map. (P.Kingston)

6.   The station had the suffix MIDLAND from 29th May 1950 until 4th May 1970, just after the Eastern Region (ex-LNER) line had closed. It became part of the London Midland Region in 1958. The route is on the right of map III. Seen in 1964 is the long up through platform, then No. 2. Its line was "Up Slow"; next was "Up Fast", then "Up Goods" and finally "Up & Down Engine". (Stations UK)

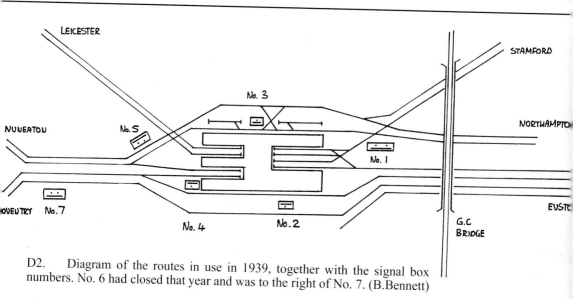

D2.   Diagram of the routes in use in 1939, together with the signal box numbers. No. 6 had closed that year and was to the right of No. 7. (B.Bennett)

7.   Further along No. 2 were the bays: No. 3 and No. 4. The latter lost its track later. Colour light signalling was introduced on the passenger lines through the station on 25th June 1939. The long task of replacing the roof began in 1992. Trains ran to Gatwick Airport from the bay on the right from June 1997. (Stations UK)

8.   Bo-Bo electric no. 86231 *Starlight Express* rattles through with a northbound express early in 1991. The lattice girder bridge in the background once carried trains from Marylebone to Sheffield, but was dismantled on Christmas Day 2006. The station roof was demolished in 2000. The 1964 Power Signal Box is glimpsed on the right. (P.Jones)

D3. Diagram to indicate the location of platforms following their renumbering in 2008. (B.Bennett)

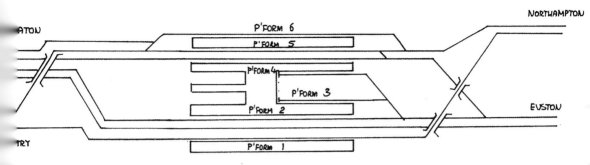

NORTHAMPTON

ATON

P'FORM 6

P'FORM 5

P'FORM 4

P'FORM 3

P'FORM 2

EUSTON

TRY

P'FORM 1

← 9. At the opposite end of the station on 22nd August 2004, a fine panorama includes, from left to right, nos 66608, 87014, 390018 and 60084. Evident are the new canopies, which replaced the old roof. A new platform on the south side came into use on 29th May 2007 as No. 1 and an island on the north side opened on 27th August 2008, as Nos 5 and 6. (M.J.Stretton)

10. We move along the car park slightly and minutes later see the "Pendolino" no. 390018 fully. It was working the 14.48 Northampton to Liverpool service from platform 2 (formerly No. 1). The foregound had once been part of the goods yard. The 2004 signalling centre is on the left and a multi-storey car park was built in 2010. (M.J.Stretton)

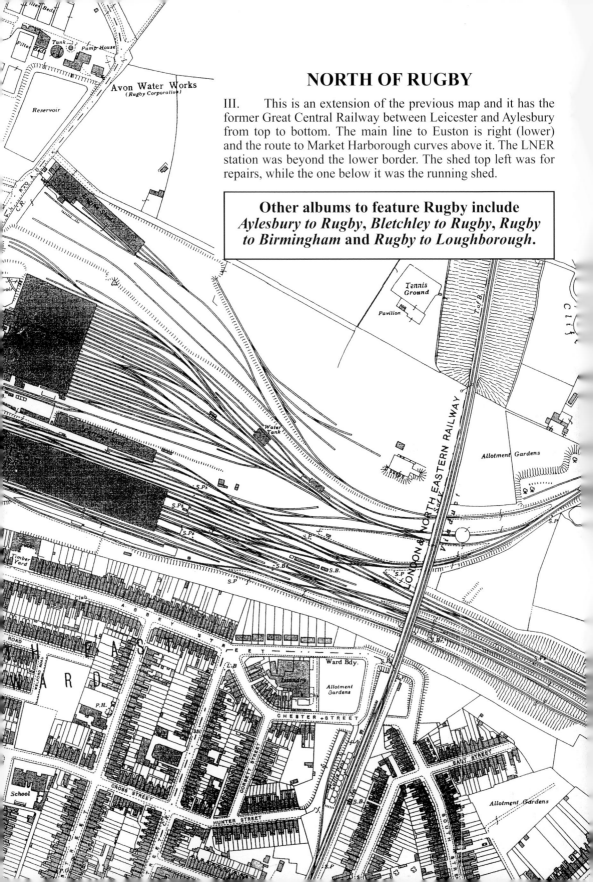

NORTH OF RUGBY

III.   This is an extension of the previous map and it has the former Great Central Railway between Leicester and Aylesbury from top to bottom. The main line to Euston is right (lower) and the route to Market Harborough curves above it. The LNER station was beyond the lower border. The shed top left was for repairs, while the one below it was the running shed.

Other albums to feature Rugby include
Aylesbury to Rugby, Bletchley to Rugby, Rugby to Birmingham **and** *Rugby to Loughborough.*

11. The repair shed is in the background, as locomotives await their turn for attention on 20th July 1935. Nearest is 0-6-0 no. 8145, a Webb "Coal Engine". This type was built in 1873-92. (H.C.Casserley)

12. The running shed had eleven roads and was photographed in March 1953. It was rebuilt and reroofed in 1955, when it was coded 2A. It became 1F in 1963. The allocations were: 106 in 1950, 59 in 1959 and only 14 in 1965. (B.W.L.Brooksbank)

13. Outside the repair shop on 13th June 1959 was another elderly ex-LNWR "Coal Engine". It provided steam to the workshop for driving the machines and for heating. Both sheds were closed on 25th May 1965. (P.Kingston)

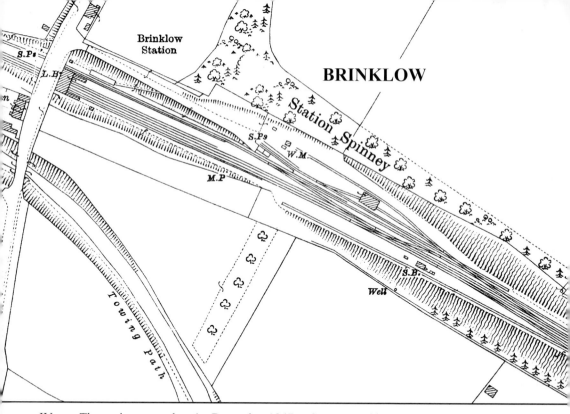

IV.   The station opened on 1st December 1847 as Stretton and became Brinklow on 1st January 1870. The latter housed 632 souls in 1901 and 1092 in 1961. The 1925 survey includes the third running line, but with only part of the fourth, which ended here.

14.   Bound for London in the 1930s is "Claughton" class 4-6-0 *Princess Louise*, with "The Mancunian". The camera is in front of the signal box. (R.M.Casserley coll.)

15.   No. 5709 *Implacable* hauls a mixture of coaches forming an up express, sometime in 1938. The booking office was at road level. (G.Coltas/M.J.Stretton coll.)

16.   Unlike the east elevation, aesthetics had been considered on these faces, with polychromatic bricks and fine tracery in the canopy design. The BR lorry is an Austin and is seen in August 1952. The road had been the Fosse Way in Roman times and the A4114 in 1919. (P.Kingston)

17.   The station is seen shortly before its closure, which was on 16th September 1957. In the distance is the small goods yard, which was in use until 20th February 1961. Also visible is the 28-lever signal box, which was closed on 13th September 1964. Further south was Newbold Box, which had 15 levers and lasted until 30th August 1964. (W.A.Camwell/SLS coll.)

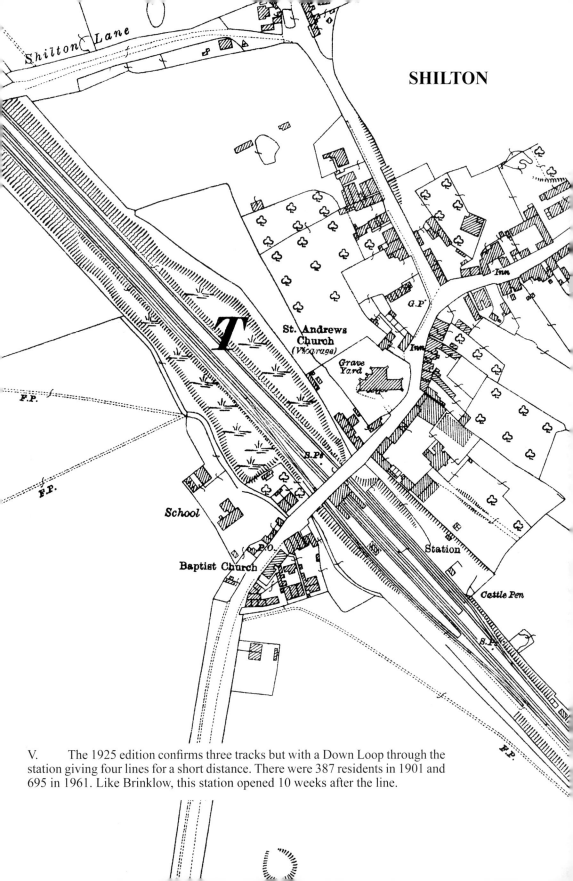

Shilton Lane

SHILTON

Inn

G.P

St. Andrews
Church
(Vicarage)

Inn

*Grave
Yard*

F.P.

F.P.

S.P.

School

P.O.

Baptist Church

Station

Cattle Pen

S.P.

F.P.

V.   The 1925 edition confirms three tracks but with a Down Loop through the
station giving four lines for a short distance. There were 387 residents in 1901 and
695 in 1961. Like Brinklow, this station opened 10 weeks after the line.

18. We start with two postcard views, this one including two signal sighting boards, Two tall signal posts and a tall bridge in the distance. (Lens of Sutton coll.)

19. A later card includes the new down island platform and signals for calling on goods trains. The cattle pens are also evident. (Lens of Sutton coll.)

→ 20. A southward panorama from 7th June 1954 confirms the lack of shelter for up passengers. Unusually, this platform has steps at one end, instead of a ramp. Another unusual detail was fencing between the siding and the running line. (P.Glenn/R.S.Carpenter)

→ 21. Seen on the same day is an up express of MkI coaches, with a down one in the distance. This is passing the end of the short four track section. The signal box is in the distance, its 24-lever frame being in use until 20th October 1963. This was the former No. 1 box; No. 2, 1,000yds to the north, had closed on 20th November 1949. (P.Glenn/R.S.Carpenter)

22.   The fireman is working hard as no. 46122 *Royal Ulster Rifleman* rushes through with "The Mancunian" on 30th August 1956. Some patchwork had been undertaken on the building. (P.Kingston)

23.   Set in stone is SHILTON STATION in this 1956 view. Luckily the vandals could not remove any letter. Closure came on 16th September 1957. The road had been the A46 since 1919, but is now the B4065. (P.Kingston)

24.   More loose boards were evident on 5th September 1957, as 4-6-0 no. 45198 trundles along with mixed freight. The second vehicle was for cattle; it received less jerking if it was close to the engine. (R.M.Casserley coll.)

25.   No. 45093 worked the last down scheduled stopping train, but few others witnessed it. The goods yard was in use until 1st February 1965. (D.A.Johnson)

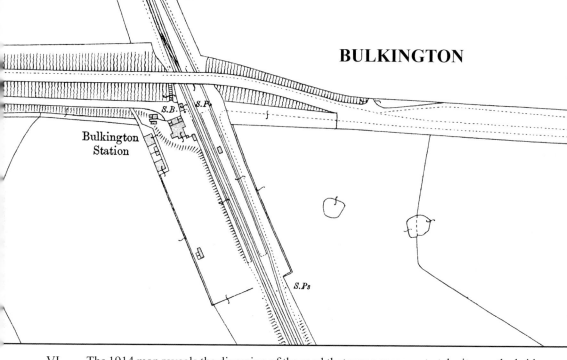

BULKINGTON

Bulkington
Station

VI.   The 1914 map reveals the diversion of the road that was necessary to take it over the bridge. The village grew from 1548 folk in 1901 to 4950 in 1961, but it was a mile from the station.

26.   The station is seen on 7th June 1954, but it had closed on 18th May 1931. The name was indelible and would have been invaluable to those travelling in open wagons on opening day. (P.Glenn/R.S.Carpenter)

27.   Recorded on the same day was no. 46236 *City of Bradford*, which was speeding through with the up "Royal Scot". The signal box closed on 14th April 1957. Over 1100yds to the north was Forders Siding of the London Brick Company, which passed beneath the main line to serve Marston Hall quarry, on the west side in use from 1904 until the 1960s. (P.Glenn/R.S.Carpenter)

28.   The line from the south was almost level, but it dropped at 1 in 320 behind the camera. The colour light signal had arrived in 1957. Over 2 miles to the north was the 20-lever Attleborough signal box, until 20th October 1963. (W.A.Camwell/SLS coll.)

29.   Recorded on 5th September 1957 was no. 44876, one of the successful class 5 4-6-0s introduced in 1934. Also evident are the steps up to the road; there were none on the up side, passengers crossing the lines on the level. (R.M.Casserley coll.)

SOUTH OF NUNEATON

30.   The shed was photographed in 1957, along with a train on the Leicester route. The codes were 2D to 1950, 2B to 1963 and 5E until closure on 6th June 1966. The allocation in 1950 was 73 locomotives, of which 22 were 0-8-0s. By 1965, the total was down to 37. (P.Kingston)

VII. Our route is from the lower right to the top on this 1914 map. Lower left is the line from Coventry, while curving to the right are the tracks to Hinckley. Near the bottom is a gated private siding.

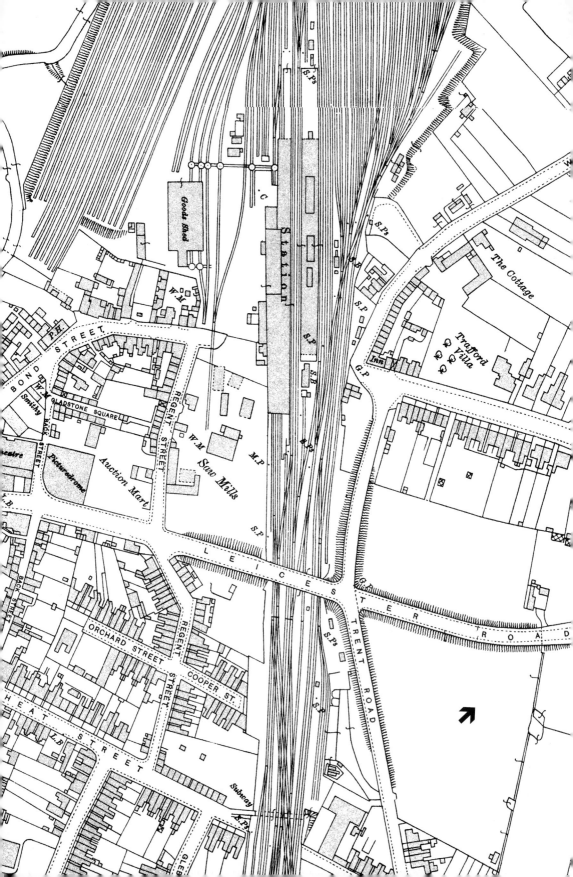

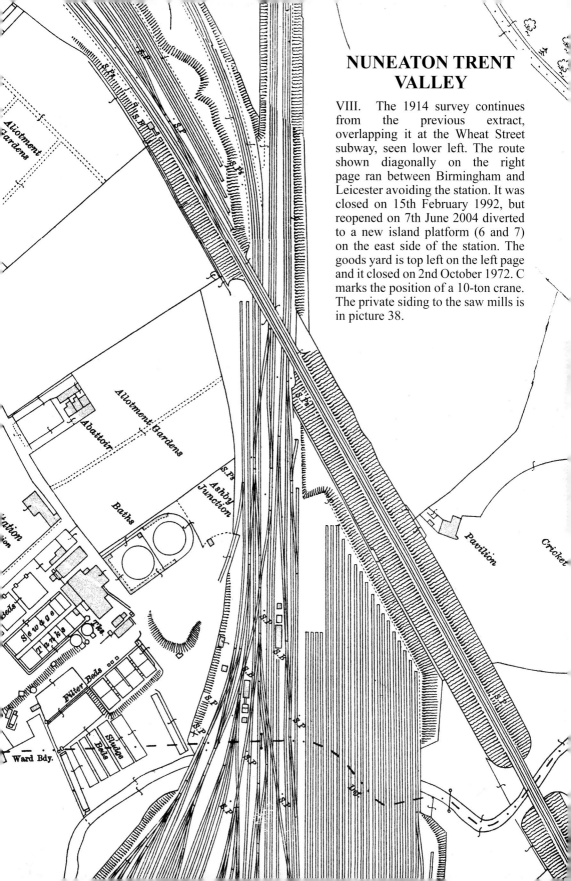

NUNEATON TRENT VALLEY

VIII. The 1914 survey continues from the previous extract, overlapping it at the Wheat Street subway, seen lower left. The route shown diagonally on the right page ran between Birmingham and Leicester avoiding the station. It was closed on 15th February 1992, but reopened on 7th June 2004 diverted to a new island platform (6 and 7) on the east side of the station. The goods yard is top left on the left page and it closed on 2nd October 1972. C marks the position of a 10-ton crane. The private siding to the saw mills is in picture 38.

Allotment Gardens

Allotment Gardens

Abattoir

Baths

Ashby Junction

Pavilion

Cricket

Sewage Tanks

Filter Beds

Sludge Beds

Ward Bdy.

31.   A view south from the main up platform in around 1910 includes a train from Coventry in the gloom on the enclosed bay platform (right). Sadly the postcard has been copied badly. A refreshment room was opened in 1888.
(Lens of Sutton coll.)

32.   An interesting shot from the south end of the up platform shows hump shunting in progress. The wagons have all been uncoupled and the one on the left is gaining speed and will be diverted into the appropriate sorting siding. Leicester Road bridge is in the background.
(R.M.Casserley coll.)

33.   It is 12th May 1937 and an unusual unit arrived. It was an Armstrong Siddeley experimental diesel-electric railcar. It was built near Coventry in 1936, one of two. They were painted red and cream and weighed 11 tons each. Both were scrapped in 1945, despite their popularity. The shield indicates that it was Coronation Day.
(Lens of Sutton coll.)

34.   With Leicester Road bridge in the background, 2-6-2T no. 205 waits to run south on 14th June 1947. The proud LMS would then exist for less than seven months more. Don't miss its ground signal. (H.C.Casserley)

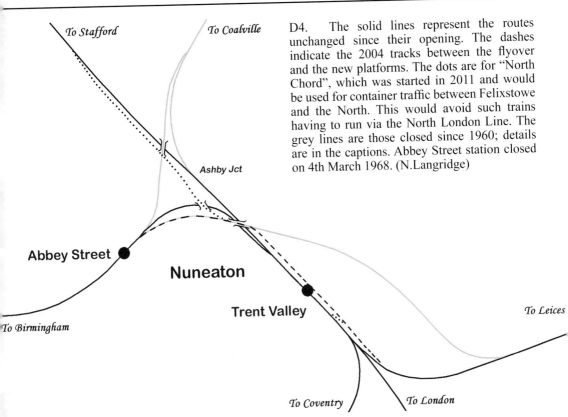

To Stafford

To Coalville

Ashby Jct

Abbey Street

Nuneaton

Trent Valley

To Birmingham

To Coventry

To London

To Leices

D4.   The solid lines represent the routes unchanged since their opening. The dashes indicate the 2004 tracks between the flyover and the new platforms. The dots are for "North Chord", which was started in 2011 and would be used for container traffic between Felixstowe and the North. This would avoid such trains having to run via the North London Line. The grey lines are those closed since 1960; details are in the captions. Abbey Street station closed on 4th March 1968. (N.Langridge)

35.   One of the many 0-8-0s based here was no. 49115. It was photographed in the late 1950s near Up Sidings Box. This had 39 levers and was reduced to a shunt frame on 6th October 1963, finally closing in August 1976. (Milepost 92½/R.S.Carpenter)

36.   An atmospheric and impromptu shot in 1957 features admirers having a thrill as 4-6-0 no. 44711 creeps through. Note that gas lighting still prevailed. (Stations UK)

37.   A panorama from Leicester Road in 1957 includes the hump (right) featured in picture 32. The entrance clock tower is on the left and in the next picture. It still stands. (Stations UK)

38.   An Austin A40 adds to the record of the entrance in 1960, as do the substantial gate pillars. Pity the two lamps had gone. The suffix TRENT VALLEY was in use from 2nd June 1924 until 5th May 1969. The former MR station closed in 1968 and all Birmingham to Leicester trains called here subsequently. (D.A.Johnson coll.)

39.   Cattle wagons lead as 4-6-0 no. 44875 leaves the up marshalling yard on 19th February 1960. On the left is a row of four shunting signals and nearer centre is No. 2 box. It had a 40-lever frame and closed on 29th January 1961. Nuneaton Power Box was in use south of the station from 6th October 1963 until 23rd August 2008. (Millbrook House)

40.   An express bound for Euston approaches on 16th January 1965, hauled by a class 40 diesel. It is entering platform No. 4, which would take 17 coaches, as would No. 2, extreme left. No. 3 took 15. (A.Wescott/R.S.Carpenter)

41.   Seen at the south end of the station on 24th July 1983 is Fison's weedkiller train. At the rear are the tankers, which are propelled by no. 25086. On the right is no. 47315. (A.C.Hartless)

42.   The crew of the 17.30 to Lichfield chat on 1st December 1984, having forgotten to change the destination blind. Unit no. 304045 had recently been reduced from four to three cars. (A.C.Hartless)

43.   The new platforms are seen on 2nd September 2011 from No. 5. Standing at No. 6 is no. 170113, which is working the 09.21 Stansted Airport to Birmingham New Street Cross Country service. (J.Whitehouse)

44.   The new lift shaft for platforms 6 and 7 is on the right as no. 170109 departs on the same day, while forming the 12.22 Birmingham New Street to Stansted Airport. The original route was further east and closed in 1992. (J.Whitehouse)

45.   Passing Ashby Junction Box on 5th October 1932 is "Royal Scot" class 4-6-0 no. 6166 *London Rifle Brigade* with "The Mancunian", destined for Euston. The box had 36 levers and lasted until 6th October 1963. (G.Coltas Trust)

46.   A wider view of the same location in about 1939 features no. 6221 *Queen Elizabeth* with the short lived streamlining used on the "Coronation Scot" service motive power. (R.S.Carpenter coll.)

47.　　Freight is leaving the Ashby route behind 2-6-0 no. 42854 on 7th September 1954. The line to Ashby lost its local service in 1931 and closed completely in 1971. The curved route seen closed in 1969. The stooks predate combine harvesters, which were then coming into use. (G.D.King/M.J.Stretton coll.)

48.　　Mancetter granite quarries siding was two miles north of Ashby Junction. Access was controlled by Hartshill Sidings signal box, which had 35 levers and became a shunt frame on 11th November 1962. (R.S.Carpenter coll.)

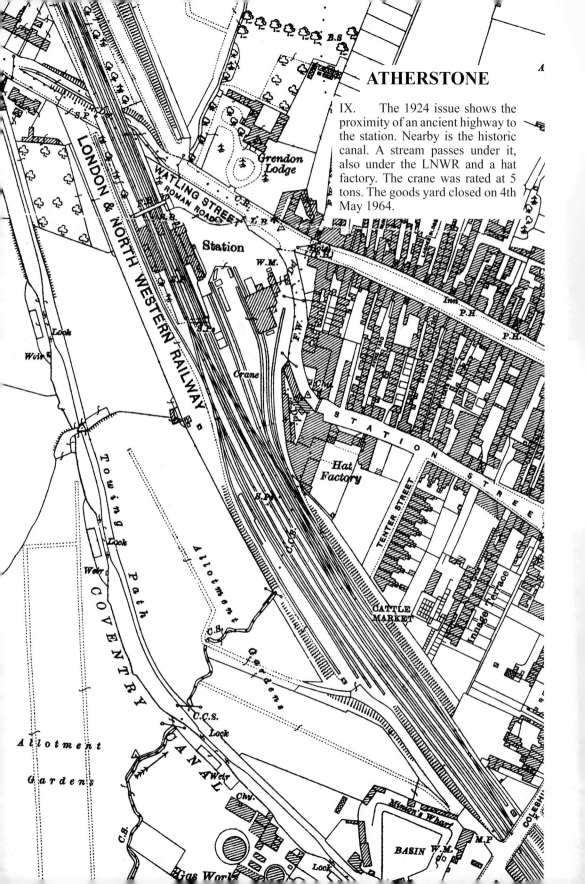

ATHERSTONE

IX.   The 1924 issue shows the proximity of an ancient highway to the station. Nearby is the historic canal. A stream passes under it, also under the LNWR and a hat factory. The crane was rated at 5 tons. The goods yard closed on 4th May 1964.

49.   A poor, but interesting, early postcard shows the down "Irish Mail" and just double track. Also of interest is the level crossing on the main A5 Holyhead road, running along the historic Watling Street here. It was replaced by a road overbridge immediately to the north of the station in September 1903. (Lens of Sutton coll.)

50.   A slightly later postcard has a more distant southward view from the new A5 road overbridge with track widening in progress; a longer up platform and a new overline type signal box is visible; it opened in 1909. (Lens of Sutton coll.)

51.   A top quality photograph from 23rd May 1961 compensates for the previous two. The signalman looks on as "Jubilee" class 4-6-0 no. 45737 *Atlas* stands with the 11.45 Liverpool to Rugby semi-fast service. The box lasted until 11th November 1962; it had 40 levers. To the north was Baddesley Sidings Box, which had 36 levers and was taken out of use on 11th November 1962. (H.Ballantyne)

52.   No. 86314 is on the down fast line on 19th April 1985 with a Dagenham to Halewood train for the Ford Motor Company. The 1962 signal box closed on 20th July 1990. It had 40 levers initially. The station was closed from 23rd May 2004 until 12th December 2005, during the modernisation work. (A.C.Hartless)

53.   We can now enjoy two photographs from 19th April 2011. No. 220103 is speeding near the historic building, while working the 11.35 from Chester to Euston; rail transport perfection indeed. The station became unstaffed on 2nd October 1972 and the fine building is now listed and in private commercial use. (A.C.Hartless)

54.   No. 350103 is arriving and forms the 10.46 Euston to Crewe. The footbridge is not what it appears to be; the right-hand steps are missing. A new entrance had been provided. This hourly service via Northampton and Stoke-on-Trent gave the town its best service ever. (A.C.Hartless)

NORTH OF ATHERSTONE

55.   The close proximity of the canal to the railway is a joy to many travellers on both systems. Passing over the Coventry Canal on 14th July 1983 are nos 25250 and 25315, while boaters wait for the lock to empty. (A.C.Hartless)

POLESWORTH

X.   The 1923 edition shows the extent of the small goods yard, which was accessed from a long headshunt. The village centre is ½ mile to the south and its residential development has now reached the railway.

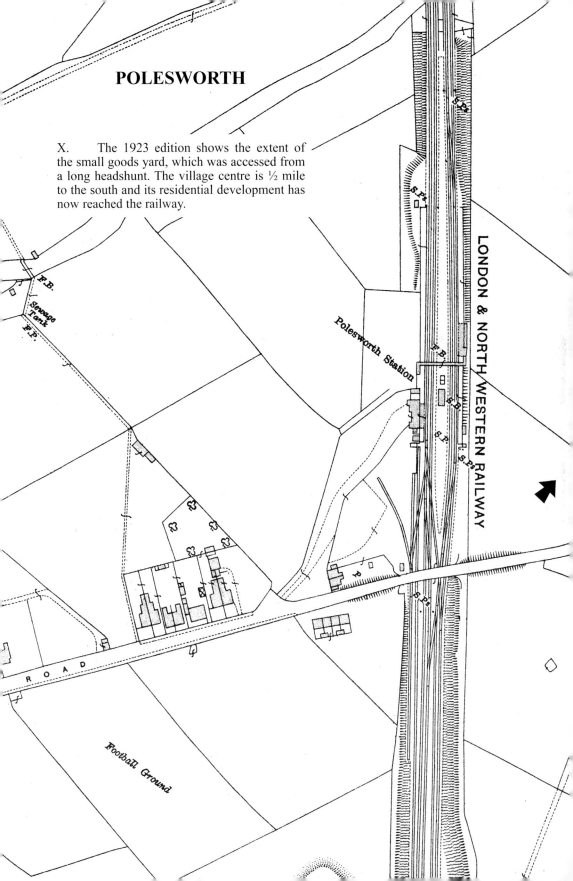

F.B.

Sewage Tank

F.P.

Polesworth Station

LONDON & NORTH WESTERN RAILWAY

S.P.

S.Ps.

S.Ps.

F.B.

F.B.

S.P.

S.Ps.

S.Ps.

P.

R O A D

Football Ground

56.   A northward panorama from the road bridge includes a one-ton crane. Space was made for an island platform, but it was never built. Marshall's Sidings signal box (36 levers) opened north of here on 29th October 1877 and closed on 25th February 1962. Beyond it was Amington Sidings box, which existed until 4th November 1962. (Stations UK)

57.   The booking office entrance is in the centre of this view from about 1949 and the front door of the house for the station master is on the left. (R.S.Carpenter coll.)

58.   An up train is about to collect a group of locals sometime in 1949. There were 4665 residents in 1901 and 4241 sixty years later. This is the view from the signal box. (R.A.Carpenter coll.)

59.   At 5.30am on 19th November 1951, the sleeping car express from Glasgow to Euston derailed on facing points, due to the excess speed of 55mph. Hauling it was class 8P 4-6-2 no. 46252 *City of Leicester* and luckily only two passengers were injured. (R.S.Carpenter coll.)

60.   Looking south in 1970, it is apparent that the track has improved, but the up side accommodation has been reduced to a bus shelter. The goods yard had closed on 7th September 1964 and staffing ceased on 2nd October 1972. (Stations UK)

61.   The down side facilities are seen in the same year, along with the new building for signalling equipment. The footbridge roof had long gone and, by 2006, there was only one train per day, a down one at 14.12. The box had 54 levers. (Stations UK)

62.   Running north on 20th June 1986 are nos 86001 and 86406 with a Tilbury to Garston Freightliner of great length. The boarded crossing was for access to the signal box, which closed on 20th July 1990. The base of its coal shed remains in place, as does a siding, but the latter would soon go. (A.C.Hartless)

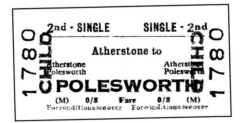

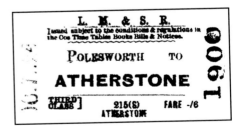

63.   The rear of no. 350124 working the 10.33 Crewe to Euston is seen on 19th April 2011. Up trains were unable to call, as the footbridge had been damaged beyond repair and had been removed in 2005. There was total closure from 23rd May 2004 to 12th December 2005. (A.C.Hartless)

64.   The abandoned up platform is seen on the same day, when only the pillars of the footbridge were present. The only train to stop here was the 06.41 Northampton to Crewe, weekdays only. (A.C.Hartless)

65.   Running near Marshall's Sidings in September 1932
is 2-6-0 no. 13152. (Bentley coll.)

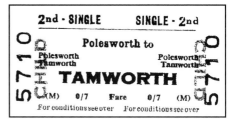

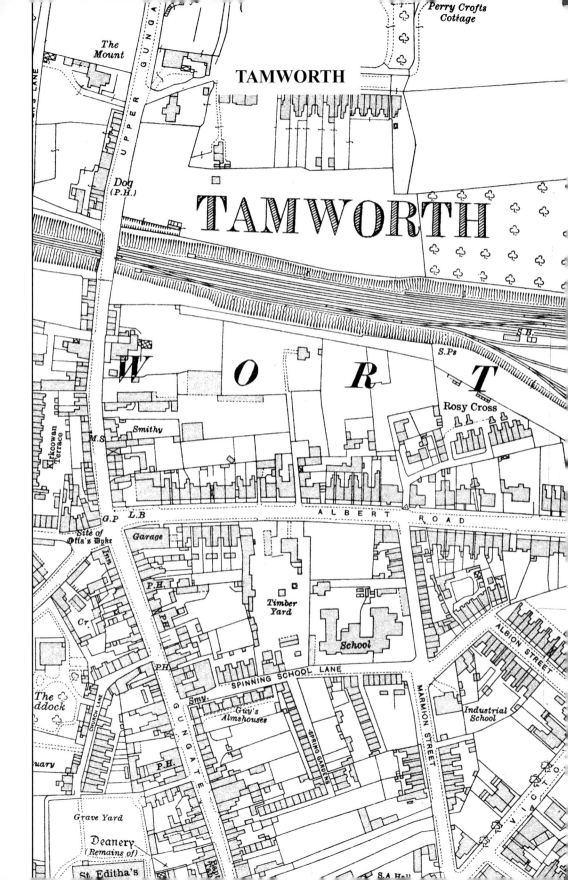

Perry Crofts
Cottage

The
Mount

TAMWORTH

UPPER GUNGA

Dog
(P.H.)

TAMWORTH

S.B.

S.Ps

W O R T

Rosy Cross

Smithy

Kirkcowan Terrace

M.S.

G.P   L.B

Site of
Offa's Dyke

Garage

ALBERT   ROAD

P.H.

Timber
Yard

Cr.

P.H.

School

ALBION STREET

The
ddock

CHURCH LANE

P.H.

GUNGATE

SPINNING SCHOOL LANE

Smy.

Guy's
Almshouses

SPRING GARDENS

MARMION STREET

Industrial
School

VICTO

uary

P.H.

Grave Yard

Deanery
(Remains of)

St. Editha's

S.A Hall

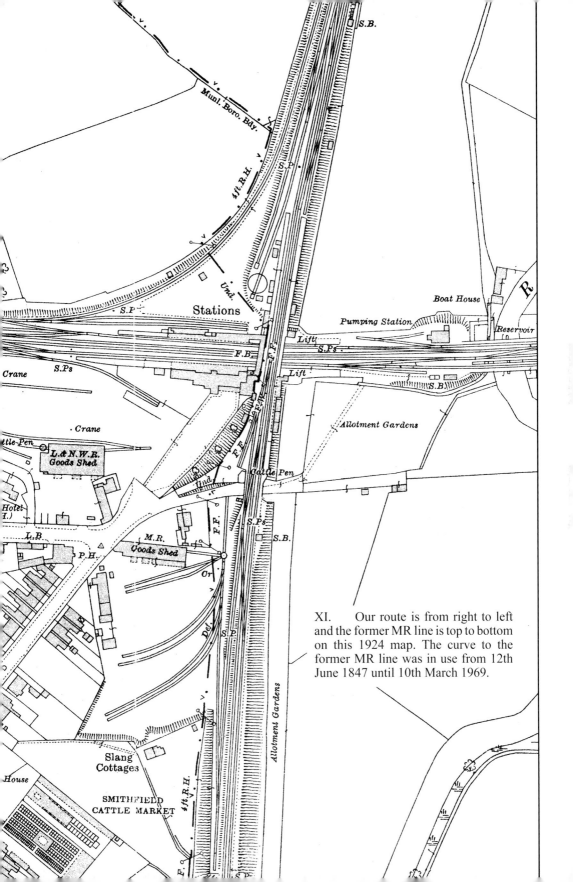

S.B.

Muni. Boro. Bdy.

4ft. R.H.

S.P.

Boat House

Stations

Und.

S.P.

Pumping Station

Reservoir

R.

Crane

S.Ps

S.P.

F.B.

F.F.

Lift

S.Ps

S.B.

Lift

Allotment Gardens

Crane

ttle-Pen

L.&.N.W.R. Goods Shed

F.F.

Und.

Cattle Pen

Hotel I.)

L.B.

P.H.

M.R. Goods Shed

F.F.

S.Ps

S.B.

Or

Del.

S.P.

XI.   Our route is from right to left and the former MR line is top to bottom on this 1924 map. The curve to the former MR line was in use from 12th June 1847 until 10th March 1969.

Slang Cottages

4ft. R.H.

House

SMITHFIELD CATTLE MARKET

Allotment Gardens

66.   The MR part of the station has mostly round head windows, whereas the LNWR ones are rectangular. Hademore water troughs were north of here. (Lens of Sutton coll.)

67.   Passing under the MR is an express from Euston hauled by "Precedent" class 2-4-0 no. 256 *President Washington*, which is piloting "Claughton" class 4-6-0 no. 154 *Captain Fryatt*. The station closed to goods traffic on 8th September 1969. (R.S.Carpenter coll.)

68.   The terms High Level and Low Level were used for the two parts of the station between 2nd June 1924 and 3rd May 1971. This view of the latter is from the former in 1950. The LNWR signal box was formerly No. 2, but was the only one at the station after No. 1 box closed on 26th May 1940. (Stations UK)

69.   The footbridge and its steps are included in this view from the same period. The signal box in the distance was called No. 1; it also appears in the next two pictures. It lasted until about 1960, but was for permanent way use only after 1940. (Stations UK)

70. The map shows the massive water tank to be close to the river, near the right border. "The Red Rose" is hauled by "Princess Royal" class 4-6-2 no. 46204 *Princess Louise* in about 1956. It will soon pass over Coton Crossing and then Hademore Crossing, where there were boxes with 25 and 15 levers respectively. They closed on 28th June 1987 and 18th March 2007, respectively. (R.S.Carpenter)

71. On the skyline in March 1957 are the former MR water tank and signal box. The white fence is next to the steps to the platform, close to a lift tower. The lifts moved large quantities of mail bags in the steam era. (R.M.Casserley)

72.   Rebuilding took place at the time of electrification, the official opening being on 24th September 1962. The simple result is seen on 2nd August 1985. No. 86417 is waiting for a down fast train to overtake it. In the distance is former No. 2 Low Level Box, which had 54 levers and was last used on 23rd August 2008. (A.C.Hartless)

73.   No. 153379 is in Regional Railways livery as it arrives on 26th April 1995, working the 15.58 Stafford to Coventry. No. 2 platform (left) would take 10 coaches, while No. 1 took 14. (D.H.Mitchell)

LICHFIELD TRENT VALLEY

74.   Bound for Euston in about 1932 is 4-6-0 no. 6141 *Caledonian*, which was later named *The North Staffordshire Regiment*. Note the covered connection between the platforms on the right. The High Level platforms closed on 18th January 1965, but reopened on 28th November 1988 for services to Birmingham and Redditch on the Cross-City Line. (R.S.Carpenter coll.)

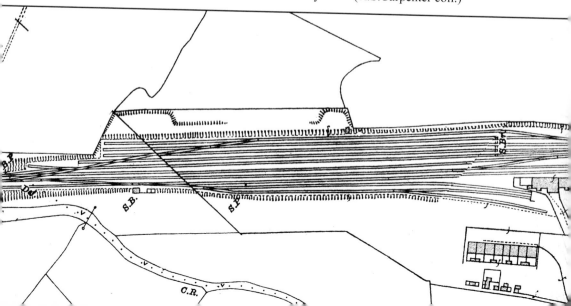

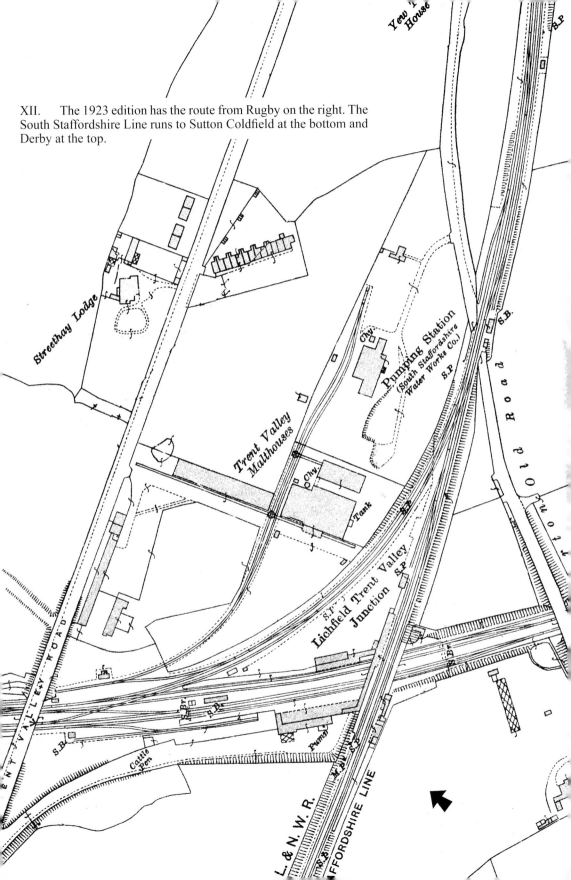

XII.   The 1923 edition has the route from Rugby on the right. The South Staffordshire Line runs to Sutton Coldfield at the bottom and Derby at the top.

Streethay Lodge

Yew
House

S.B.

Pumping Station
(South Staffordshire
Water Works Co.)

Chy.

S.P.

S.B.

Old Road

Trent Valley
Malthouses

Chy.

Tank

S.P.

Lichfield Trent Valley
Junction

S.P.

S.B.

T R E N T   V A L L E Y   R O A D

S.B.

S.B.

S.B.

S.B.

Cattle
Pen

Pump.

S.P.

L. & N. W. R.

STAFFORDSHIRE LINE

75.   This view is from Trent Valley Road bridge in about 1936 and is across the join in the map pages. It features the original station building and a siding full of cattle wagons. S.Br. on the map indicates a signal bridge. (E.S.Russell/SLS)

76.   We look north at the 1871 building, its glazed entrance being shown as diamonds on the map. No. 6202 was a 4-6-2 with turbine drive and of the "Princess Royal" class. It is working the 8.30am Euston to Liverpool. (H.C.Casserley)

77.   Working "The Comet" to Euston in about 1956 is "Patriot" class 4-6-0 no. 45540 *Sir Robert Turnbull*. The connecting curve is on the left. (R.S.Carpenter)

78.   Looking towards Stafford on 23rd March 1957, we have Trent Valley Road across the picture and the signal box is No. 1, which had 80 levers and closed on 29th May 2008. No. 2 is on the left page of the map, had 24 levers and lasted until 9th July 1962. Further north was the 12-lever Elmhurst Crossing Box, which ceased to be used on 28th October 1979. (H.C.Casserley)

79.   We are looking towards Rugby from Trent Valley Road bridge in June 1960, with the cattle pens on the right. The gated siding served the waterworks and some malthouses. A train is southbound at the High Level platform. (W.A.Camwell/SLS)

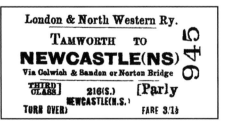

London & North Western Ry.

TAMWORTH   TO

NEWCASTLE(NS) 945

Via Colwich & Sandon or Norton Bridge

THIRD]
CLASS   216(S.)   [Parly
    NEWCASTLE(N.S.)

TURN OVER)   FARE 3/1½

London & North Western Ry.

Issued subject to the conditions & regulations in the Coy Time Tables Books Bills & Notices.

TAMWORTH   TO

RUGBY(L.&N.W.) 5

Third]   216(S)   [Class
    RUGBY

TURN OVER)   FARE 2/3½

80.   This view is from the west end prior to the platforms being extended. No. 86501 is working a Felixstowe to Crewe Freightliner on 6th June 2007. The 12 mile double-track Tamworth-Lichfield-Armitage 'bottleneck' was removed with the 4-tracking of this section in 2008. (J.Whitehouse)

81.   Extreme economy was employed for a new booking office at the time of electrification. Burton Road bridge is in the background on 29th August 2011 in this view of the downside. (J.Whitehouse)

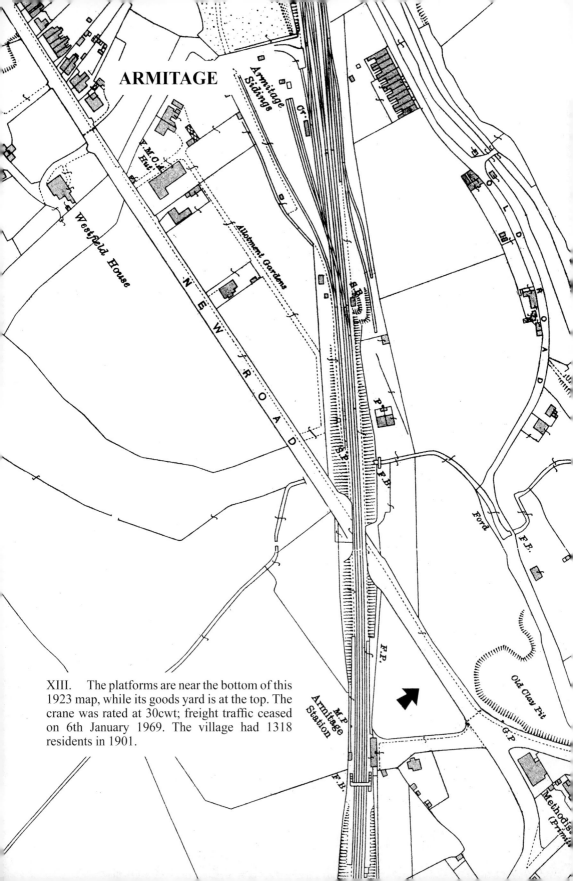

ARMITAGE

Westfield House

NEW ROAD

M.O.W. Hut

Armitage Sidings

Allotment Gardens

Cr.

S.B.

P.

S.P.

F.B.

P.

Ford

F.P.

F.P.

M.P. Armitage Station

F.B.

Old Clay Pit

G.P.

F.P.

F.P.

Methodis (Primi

XIII.   The platforms are near the bottom of this 1923 map, while its goods yard is at the top. The crane was rated at 30cwt; freight traffic ceased on 6th January 1969. The village had 1318 residents in 1901.

82.   A departing train was an unusual subject for a postcard, as was the pump for filling the fire buckets and those for a more personal use. The station was used by passengers from 1st December 1847 until 13th June 1960. (Lens of Sutton coll.)

83.   A northward view in about 1939 includes three telegraph routes. The left signal arm is for the loop, which started close to the signal box (S.B. on the map). This had 25 levers and was closed on 29th March 1970; it was nicknamed "Toilet Basin Junction" due to the proximity of the large bathroomware factory of Armitage-Shanks nearby. (Stations UK)

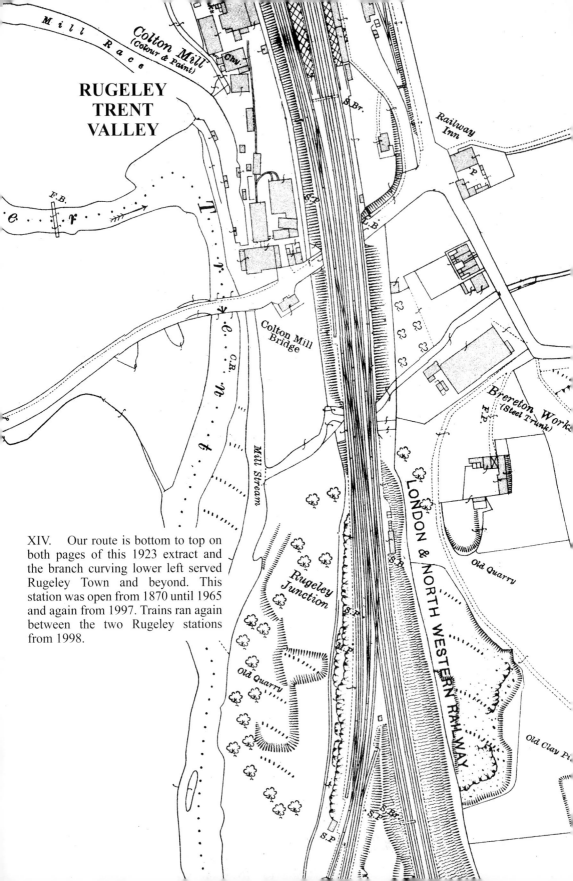

RUGELEY TRENT VALLEY

Colton Mill
(Colour & Paint)

Mill Race

F.B.

S.Br.

S.P.

S.B.

Railway Inn

Colton Mill Bridge

Mill Stream

Brereton Works
(Steel Trunk)

F.P.

Old Quarry

Rugeley Junction

S.P.

LONDON & NORTH WESTERN RAILWAY

Old Quarry

Old Clay Pi

S.P.

S.Br.

XIV. Our route is bottom to top on both pages of this 1923 extract and the branch curving lower left served Rugeley Town and beyond. This station was open from 1870 until 1965 and again from 1997. Trains ran again between the two Rugeley stations from 1998.

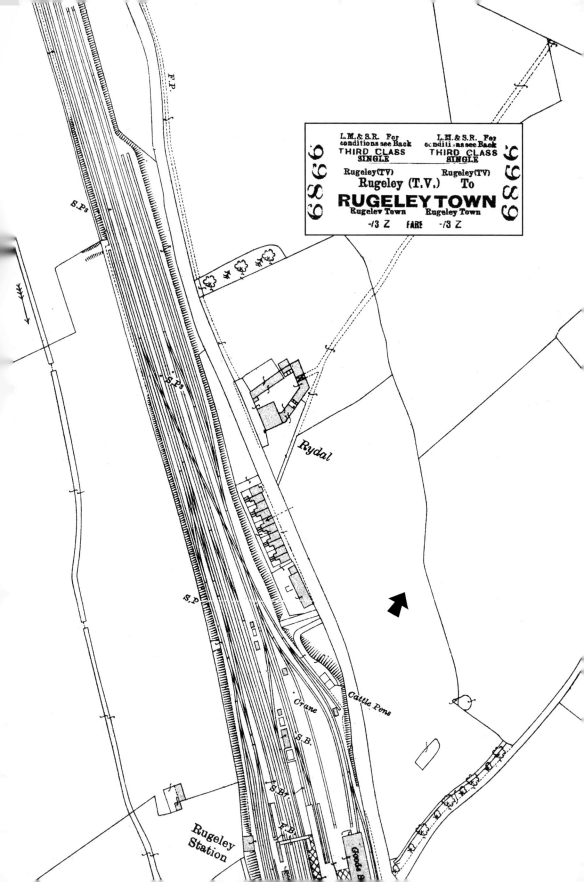

L.M.&S.R. For L.M.&S.R. For
conditions see Back conditions see Back
THIRD CLASS **THIRD CLASS**
SINGLE SINGLE

Rugeley(TV) Rugeley(TV)
Rugeley (T.V.) To

RUGELEY TOWN

Rugeley Town Rugeley Town

-/3 Z FARE -/3 Z

6989 6989

F.P.

S.P.s

S.P.s

S.P.

Rydal

Cattle Pens

Crane

S.B.

S.B.

S.Bx.

F.B.

Rugeley
Station

Goods B

84.   This shows the first station and signal box. The signal arm went through a slot in the post. This was the era when sleepers could be covered with ballast. (R.S.Carpenter coll.)

85.   The suffix TRENT VALLEY was officially in use from 1st June 1870 until 6th May 1968. This suggests that this is a pre-1870 print. The words were used again from 11th May 1992. (Lens of Sutton coll.)

86.   The lengthened canopy is evident as a 4-4-0 brings in a Stafford-Rugby local service on 26th May 1956. (W.A.Camwell/SLS)

87.   Looking south in 1957, we see another massive water tank and close to it are three long loop lines used for holding goods trains when expresses needed to pass them. (Stations UK)

88.　　One such freight service rumbles south on the fast line in the late 1950s. The locomotive is 2-6-0 no. 42920 of class 6P5F, a type introduced in 1926. The up platform took seven coaches, No. 2 five and No. 1 four. (R.S.Carpenter)

89.　　On the right is the goods yard, which closed on 4th July 1966; it had a 5-ton crane. This northward view is from 19th September 1959 and features the 80-lever No. 2 Box, which lasted until 18th August 1974. No. 1 was at Rugeley Junction, had 75 levers and closed on 17th November 1974. (H.C.Casserley)

90.   A new and taller footbridge was required for adequate clearance for the 25kV wires. No. 87016 *Sir Francis Drake* is running to Euston on 29th July 1978, with the obligatory luggage van next to the locomotive. No buildings survived here; staffing ceased on 2nd October 1972. (T.Heavyside)

91.   Seen on the same day is no. 87029 *Earl Marischal* with a down train from London. The line to the right of it is bidirectional and to the right of that is a loop. Both are electrified for a short distance on the curve from which sidings enter the massive Rugeley 'B' Power Station, seen in the background. Platform 1 is in the foreground; 2 and 3 are in picture 90, left and right. (T.Heavyside)

COLWICH

92.   We look towards the 55-lever box, which was in use until 28th May 1961. The parcels shed is on the left. The number of residents nearby rose from 1443 in 1901 to 1844 in 1961. (Lens of Sutton coll.)

XV.   The 1923 map has the route to Stoke-on-Trent curving away, left upper, with the exchange sidings nearby. The goods yard is south of the main line, east of the station. Its name has a silent W.

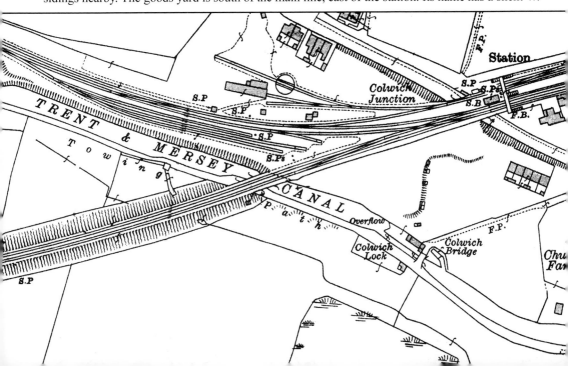

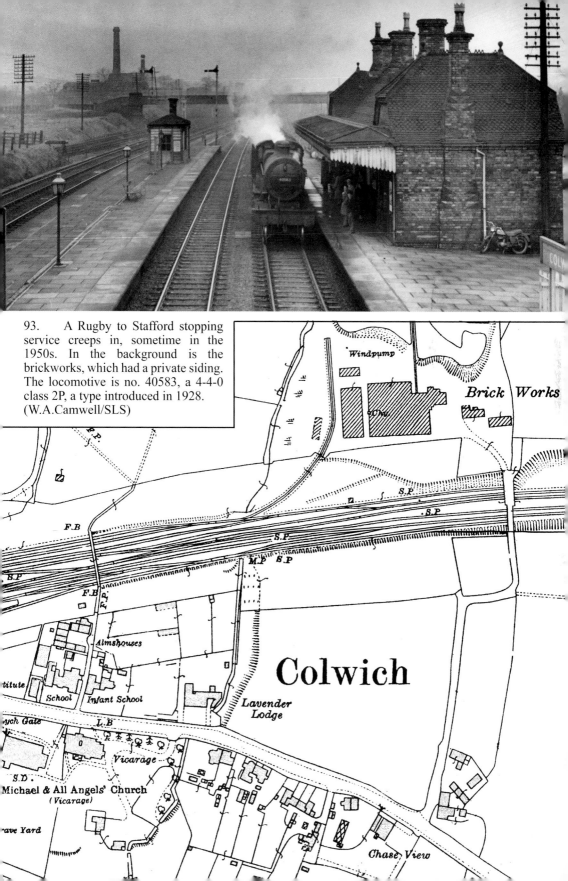

93.   A Rugby to Stafford stopping service creeps in, sometime in the 1950s. In the background is the brickworks, which had a private siding. The locomotive is no. 40583, a 4-4-0 class 2P, a type introduced in 1928. (W.A.Camwell/SLS)

94.   One of the two goods sidings is close to the Nissen hut in this shot from 20th September 1959. Freight and passenger services had been withdrawn on 3rd February 1958. (H.C.Casserley)

95.   The footbridge is the one in picture 93 and thus the location of the new signal box can be easily established. Freight from the Walsall area is behind class 4F 0-6-0 no. 44226 on 4th November 1961. (Milepost 92½)

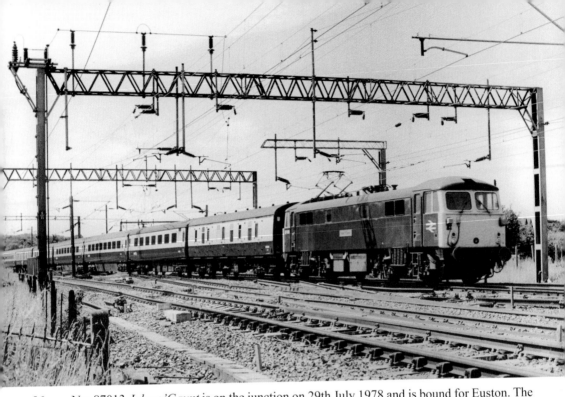

96.   No. 87013 *John o'Gaunt* is on the junction on 29th July 1978 and is bound for Euston. The four tracks diverge into two pairs of two here. (T.Heavyside)

97.   A panorama from the footbridge on 2nd April 2005 has the former North Staffs Railway curving to the right and the former station building on the left. The 45 levers of the 1961 box were reduced to 30 in 1974, when a panel was added. Closure came on 12th June 2005. (H.Ballantyne)

98.   Shugborough Tunnel is 1½ miles from the junction and is 777yds long. A Euston express is emerging from it on 17th August 1974. (T.Heavyside)

99.　　Slightly nearer to it in July 1933 is a local train hauled by an unnamed "Prince of Wales" class 4-6-0. The hut was for the fogman, who would apply detonators to the rail as necessary. (R.M.Casserley coll.)

100.　　Emerging from the more ornate west portal in June 1954 is "The Mancunian", hauled by "Royal Scot" class 4-6-0 no. 46158 *The Loyal Regiment*. The tunnel avoided the line cutting through Shugborough Park, the property of the Earl of Lichfield, hence the careful attention paid to the design of its portals. (R.M.Casserley coll.)

MILFORD & BROCTON

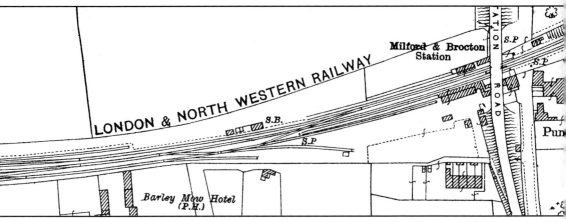

XVI.   The 1923 edition shows the small goods yard, which closed on 7th March 1960. The tiny village of Milford was close by, but the larger one of Brocton was about one mile to the south. The station opened on 18th May 1877, immediately west of Tixall Crossing, which was later closed.

SOUTH OF STAFFORD

101.   The words CANNOCK CHASE were added in about 1933 and this photograph was taken soon after. The new bridge span was for a third track. Closure came on 6th March 1950 for passengers. Behind the camera is the 36-lever signal box, which closed on 12th June 1977. Two miles north was Baswich signal box (20 levers), controlling access to a saltworks siding; it closed on 20th May 1962 and was replaced by a ground frame. (Stations UK)

102.   This is Queensville Curve and no. 86017 is bound for Euston on 29th July 1978. The sidings are just beyond the right border of the next map and were used by the engineers. Queensville Box had 25 levers and was in use until 3rd April 1977. Sidings on the up side at Queensville served the English Electric (later GEC) factory, whilst opposite the British Reinforced Concrete Engineering Company had sidings. Both firms ceased to be rail served during the 1980s. (T.Heavyside)

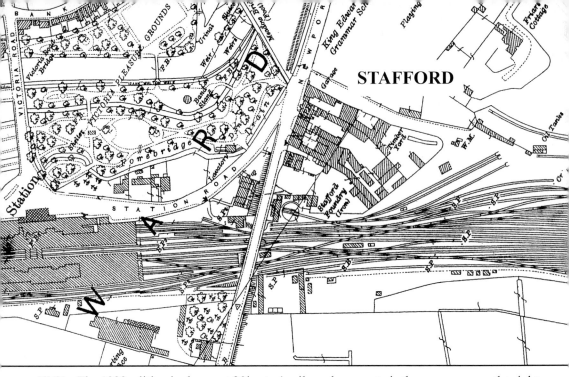

XVII. The 1923 edition is shown at 20ins to 1 mile and our route is the upper one on the right. Below it is the 1837 main line from Wolverhampton. No. 1 Box is within the junction on the right and No. 2 is near the corner of Telegraph Street. No. 4 is to the right of the bridge on the left page. It seems that No. 3 was short lived; located opposite No. 4 box, it controlled the up sidings north end.

103. Keeping its smoke clear of the overall roof in 1904 is 4-4-0 no. 1952 *Benbow*. This is a Webb compound of the "Alfred the Great" class. The crossing seems in poor condition. The Great Northern Railway ran to Burton-on-Trent and its separate booking office was retained until about 1932. (R.S.Carpenter coll.)

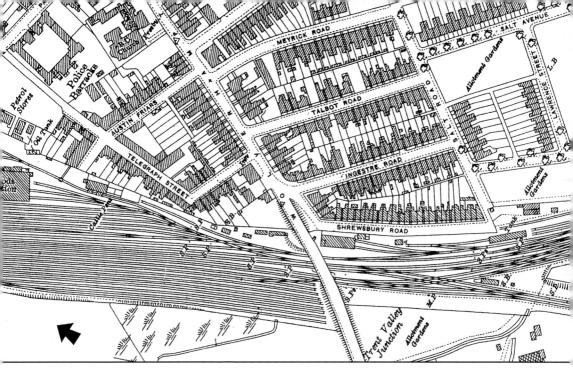

104.   A panorama from the mid-1920s gives a good impression of the fragmented development of the station. The original 1837 Grand Junction Station was replaced in 1844. Further reconstruction in 1861-2 saw a new station slightly to the north, with two main platforms surmounted by 'Euston' type hipped roofs, with bays at each end. (Stations UK)

105.   A southward view from the western platform reveals that there was a scissors crossover to allow two trains to use it simultaneously. This platform face was provided in the early 1880s, converting the down platform into an island. (R.M.Casserley coll.)

106.   Most of the glazing was lost during the air raids of World War II, as seen in this 1949 photograph. The photographer is looking north from Newport Road bridge, which is in the background of the next picture. (Stations UK)

107. Parcels were prolific in 1949. A tea can was usually found in the hand of a locoman. The two through roads are in the open. (Stations UK)

108. Looking north from the station, No. 5 signal box is visible against Bagnall's bridge. Pictured on 11th July 1949 is "Coronation" class 4-6-2 no. 46251 *City of Nottingham* arriving, bound for Euston. (D.H.Mitchell coll.)

109. Northbound on the same day is class 5 4-6-0 no. 44892. The absence of roofing over the fast lines reduced the amount of smoke collecting in the station. (D.H.Mitchell coll.)

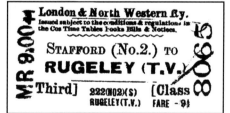

London & North Western Ry.
Issued subject to the conditions & regulations in the Cos Time Tables Books Bills & Notices.
STAFFORD (No.2.) TO
RUGELEY (T.V.)
Third] 222(N02)(S) [Class
RUGELEY(T.V.) FARE - 9½

MR 9.004
8065

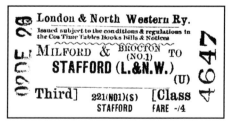

London & North Western Ry.
Issued subject to the conditions & regulations in the Cos Time Tables Books Bills & Notices
MILFORD & BROCTON (NO.1) TO
STAFFORD (L.&N.W.) (U)
Third] 221(N01)(S) [Class
STAFFORD FARE -/4

4647

London & North Western Ry
STAFFORD
7 PLATFORM.
This Ticket must be given up when leaving the Station or at the time of booking.

B 7811

L.M.&S.R. FOR CONDITIONS SEE BACK
PARKING TICKET FOR
MOTOR CAR or
THREE-WHEELED VEHICLE
AT
STAFFORD(LMS)
Valid for 7 Days
ending
Registration No. BSH 571
Fee 2/6 P

800 800

110.   Running in from the south under Newport Road is 2-6-0 no. 42815. Note the calling-on signals on the right. The signal box in the background is No. 4. No. 2 had a 36-lever frame and was closed on 30th January 1972. No. 1 box at Trent Valley Junction had 112 levers and closed on 31st March 1974. (D.H.Mitchell coll.)

111.   It is April 1952 and 4-6-0 no. 45514 *Holyhead* is departing south and has been signalled for the Wolverhampton route. (G.Coltas Trust)

112.   Reconstruction began early in 1960 and the new station was officially opened on 31st December 1962. It had five through platforms. The new No. 4 signal box (105 levers) opened on 4th December 1960 and was still in use in 2011. It had replaced the previous No. 4 box (opened on 4th February 1934), which is seen in photograph 110. (Railway Magazine)

→ 113.   We can now enjoy two action shots from 14th April 1960 from Newport Road. Class 5MT 2-6-0 no. 42931 is working a class C freight. The leading wagon carries an early container. (B.W.L.Brooksbank)

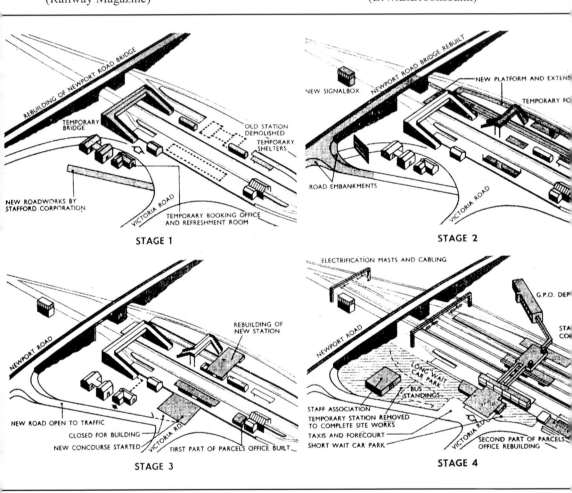

STAGE 1

STAGE 2

STAGE 3

STAGE 4

→   114.   Running south is another class 5MT, this time no. 45097. It is hauling an up relief express and the second coach is near one of the new colour light signals. (B.W.L.Brooksbank)

115.   This rare view north from the temporarily exposed footbridge is from September 1960 during reconstruction of the station. The signal box is No. 6 which closed on 7th May 1961. In the left background is the engine shed and the lofty coaling plant. (D.K.Jones coll.)

116.   No. 24082 is working an engineers train from the Crewe direction on 29th July 1978 and has just run under Wolverhampton Road bridge. The signal box behind the train is No. 5, which opened on 18th February 1952 (150 levers) replacing the old LNWR box (photograph 108) and was still in use in 2011. (T.Heavyside)

117.   Noted locomotive builders in Stafford were W.G.Bagnall Ltd from 1870 to 1951, when they merged with Brush Traction Ltd. In 1959, they became part of W.H.Dorman Ltd and in 1961 part of English Electric. The factory closed at that time and this 1897 product was put on display later. Named *Isobel*, it is seen outside the station in 1978; it was later moved to the nearby Amerton Railway. (T.Heavyside)

118.   Class 322 units passed through for 12 months in 1998-99 only, but the 325s (as seen) were more faithful. These were built specifically for postal traffic and were photographed on 22nd February 2001 running empty from Crewe to Willesden. These EMUs were still in use in 2011 for several postal trains daily between London, Warrington and Glasgow. (D.H.Mitchell)

119.   An unusual visitor on 13th April 2005 was the Network Rail measurement train. It is an HST unit painted entirely yellow and is running from Crewe to Euston, via the Trent Valley line. (H.Ballantyne)

120.   A new platform was opened on 24th May 1997 to serve the Royal Mail depot on the down side (out of view to the right of this photograph). A "Train Spotters" room was established in 1999 by Virgin Trains. We are looking south on 15th June 2006, when passenger traffic figures were continuing to rise. They doubled in the 14 years to 2011 on this main line. (B.W.L.Brooksbank)

MP Middleton Press

EVOLVING THE ULTIMATE RAIL ENCYCLOPEDIA

Easebourne Lane, Midhurst, West Sussex.
GU29 9AZ Tel:01730 813169

www.middletonpress.co.uk email:info@middletonpress.co.uk
A-978 0 906520 B- 978 1 873793 C- 978 1 901706 D-978 1 904474
E- 978 1 906008 F - 978 1 908174

All titles listed below were in print at time of publication - please check current availability by looking at our website - *www.middletonpress.co.uk* or by requesting a Brochure which includes our *LATEST* RAILWAY TITLES also our TRAMWAY, TROLLEYBUS, MILITARY and WATERWAYS series